HOW TO DO

THE

BALANCED

WORKAHOLIC

Discover The Trick To Being
Incredibly Productive Yet Have
Plenty of Time For Fun

Robin Lewis

Table of Contents

PART 1

Chapter 1:

Trust The Process

Today we're going to talk about the power of having faith that things will work out for you even though you can't see the end in sight just yet. And why you need to simply trust in the process in all the things that you do.

Fear is something that we all have. We fear that if we quit our jobs to pursue our passions, that we may not be able to feed ourselves if our dreams do not work out. We fear that if we embark on a new business venture, that it might fail and we would have incurred financial and professional setbacks.

All this is borne out of the fear of the unknown. The truth is that we really do not know what can or will happen. We may try to imagine in our heads as much as we can, but we can never really know until we try and experienced it for ourselves.

The only way to overcome the fear of the unknown is to take small steps, one day at a time. We will, to the best of our ability, execute the plan that we have set for ourselves. And the rest we leave it up to the confidence that our actions will lead to results.

If problems arise, we deal with it there and then. We put out fires, we implement updated strategies, and we keep going. We keep going until we have exhausted all avenues. Until there is no more roads for us to travel, no more paths for us to create. That is the best thing that we can do.

If we constantly focus on the fear, we will never go anywhere. If we constantly worry about the future, we will never be happy with the present. If we dwell on our past failures, we will be a victim of our own shortcomings. We will not grow, we will not learn, we will not get better.

I challenge each and every one of you today to make the best out of every situation that you will face. Grab fear by the horns and toss them aside as if it were nothing. I believe in you and all that you can achieve.

Chapter 2:

How To Worry Less

How many of you worry about little things that affect the way you go about your day? That when you're out with your friends having a good time or just carrying out your daily activities, when out of nowhere a sudden burst of sadness enters your heart and mind and immediately you start to think about the worries and troubles you are facing. It is like you're fighting to stay positive and just enjoy your day but your mind just won't let you. It becomes a tug of war or a battle to see who wins?

How many of you also lose sleep because your mind starts racing at bedtime and you're flooded with sad feelings of uncertainty, despair, worthlessness or other negative emotions that when you wake up, that feeling of dread immediately overwhelms you and you just feel like life is too difficult and you just dont want to get out of bed.

Well If you have felt those things or are feeling those things right now, I want to tell you you're not alone. Because I too struggle with those feelings or emotions on a regular basis.

At the time of writing this, I was faced with many uncertainties in life. My business had just ran into some problems, my stocks weren't doing well, I had lost money, my bank account was telling me I wasn't good enough, but most importantly, i had lost confidence. I had lost the ability to face each day with confidence that things will get better. I felt that i was worthless and that bad things will always happen to me. I kept seeing the negative side of things and it took a great deal of emotional toll on me. It wasn't like i chose to think and feel these things, but they just came into my mind whenever they liked. It was like a parasite feeding off my negative energy and thriving on it, and weakening me at the same time.

Now your struggles may be different. You may have a totally different set of circumstances and struggles that you're facing, but the underlying issue is the same. We all go through times of despair, worry, frustration, and uncertainty. And it's totally normal and we shouldn't feel ashamed of it but to accept that it is a part of life and part of our reality.

But there are things we can do to minimise these worries and to shift to a healthier thought pattern that increases our ability to fight off these negative emotions.

I want to give you 5 actionable steps that you can take to worry less and be happier. And these steps are interlinked that can be carried out in fluid succession for the greatest benefit to you. But of course you can choose whichever ones speaks the most to you and it is more important that you are able to practice any one of these steps consistently rather than doing all 5 of them haphazardly. But I want to make sure I give you all the tools so that you can make the best decisions for yourself.

Try this with me right now as I go through these 5 steps and experience the benefit for yourself instead of waiting until something bad happens.

The very first step is simple. Just breathe. When a terrible feeling of sadness rushes into your body out of nowhere, take that as a cue to close your eyes, stop whatever you are doing, and take 5 deep breathes through your nose. Breathing into your chest and diaphragm. Deep breathing has the physiological benefit of calming your nerves and releasing tension in the body and it is a quick way to block out your negative thoughts. Pause the video if you need to do practice your deep breathing before we move on.

And as you deep breathe, begin the second step. Which is to practice gratefulness. Be grateful for what you already have instead of what you think u need to have to be happy. You could be grateful for your dog, your family, your friends, and whatever means the most to you. And if you cannot think of anything to be grateful for, just be grateful that you are even alive and walking on this earth today because that is special and amazing in its own right.

Next is to practice love and kindness to yourself. You are too special and too important to be so cruel to yourself. You deserve to be loved and you owe it to yourself to be kind and forgiving. Life is tough as it is, don't make it harder. If you don't believe in yourself, I believe in you and I believe in your worthiness as a person that you have a lot left to give.

The fourth step is to Live Everyday as if it were your last. Ask yourself, will you still want to spend your time worrying about things out of your control if it was your last day on earth? Will you be able to forgive yourself if you spent 23 out of the last 24 hours of your life worrying? Or will you choose to make the most out of the day by doing things that are meaningful and to practice love to your family, friends, and yourself?

Finally, I just want you to believe in yourself and Have hope that whatever actions you are taking now will bear fruition in the future. That they will not be in vain. That at the end of the day, you have done everything to the very best of your ability and you will have no regrets and you have left no stone unturned.

How do you feel now? Do you feel that it has helped at least a little or even a lot in shaping how you view things now? That you can shift your perspective and focus on the positives instead of the worries?

If it has worked for you today, I want to challenge you to consistently practice as many of these 5 steps throughout your daily lives every single day. When you feel a deep sadness coming over you, come back to this video if you need guidance, or practice these steps if you remember them on your own.

I wish you only good things and I hope that I have helped you that much more today. Thank you for your supporting me and this channel and if you find that I can do more for you, do subscribe to my channel and I'll see you in the next one. Take care.

Chapter 3:

Work Harder Than Everybody Else

Lacking motivation and lacking the drive and will to get up out of our butts to take that step towards making our dreams a reality is one that everyone struggles with, even me. Every single day, I wake up knowing the plan and the steps i need to take to get where I want to be, but i just can't seem to bring myself to do these necessary tasks. It is as if a wall is blocking my mind from wanting to do the work.

That is until i came across an article highlighting the power of just working harder than everybody else in whatever field or industry you are in. That you just work harder than your peers and success will come to you. And in this article, it tells the story of how Kobe Bryant, Jack Ma, Mark Cuban, and many other highly successful CEOs and entrepreneurs have achieved immense wealth and success just by working harder than anyone else.

While this concept may seem simple, it is certainty not as easy as it sounds. Putting hours more than your peers when they could be out there relaxing, enjoying life, partying and what not is a sacrifice that not everyone is willing to make. But it is this insane work ethic that drives these people to levels of success not seen by their peers.

Kobe Bryant puts this the best. With every 4 hours more that he practices more than his peers on the basketball court everyday, it starts to add up and compound in an incredible way that by the 5th year of training, none of his peers would ever be able to catch up to him no matter how hard they trained before every tournament or championship. By the time comes around, Kobe would have clocked in thousands of hours more than his peers in practice, and what he lacks for in talent (which I doubt is a factor), he makes up for in time on the court. And this time is what makes him one of the best players of all time. Putting him in the league of legends such as Michael Jordan.

The takeaway from Kobe's story is that every minute extra that you put in more than your peers will add up in time and put you leaps and bounds better than your competition. This can be applied to any field, whether it be a real estate career, as an investor, a trader, an athlete. Anything you set aside time for, you will gain the knowledge in time. You just have to start believing in the hours that you put in will pay off eventually.

This is a lesson that I have experienced personally as well. Many of us want to achieve happiness and success fast, today, now, but they forget that greatness isn't built in a day. And I realised that many of the things that i became good at took time to nurture. And the hours i put it only started paying off 2 to 3 years from the day I began embarking on that new journey or career. and I expect that my future endeavours will also take time to grow.

It is the same as watering a baby sprout everyday and giving it sunlight and water consistently, it only starts to grow really big by its 2nd or 3rd year being a healthy plant constantly fed with nutrients to ensure it has the best chance of survival and growth.

I challenge you today to work harder than everybody else around you and have an insane work ethic. Grind it out every single day, put in the hours that is necessary until you succeed and work your face off. Dont settle for anything less and remove distractions that suck out your time. If you outwork everyone every single day, you will eventually come out on top no matter how talented your competition might be. Just give it your best and never give up.

I hope you learned something today and are taking the necessary steps to get one step closed to your dreams. I wish you success and happiness. Take care and see you in the next one.

Chapter 4:

When It Is Time To Let Go and Move On (Career)

Today we're going to talk about a topic that I hope will motivate you to quit that job that you hate or one that you feel that you have nothing more to give anymore.

For the purpose of this video, we will focus mainly on career as I believe many of you may feel as though you are stuck in your job but fear quitting because you are afraid you might not find a better one.

For today's topic, I want to draw attention to a close friend of mine who have had this dilemma for years and still hasn't decided to quit because he is afraid that he might not get hired by someone else.

In the beginning of my friend's career, he was full of excitement in his new job and wanted to do things perfectly. Things went pretty smoothly over the course of the first 2 years, learning new things, meeting new friends, and getting settled into his job that he thought he might stay on for a long time to come seeing that it was the degree that he had pursued in university. However when the 3rd year came along, he started to feel jaded with his job. Everyday he would meet ungrateful and sometimes mean customers who were incredibly self-entitled. They would be rude and he started dreading going to work more and more each day. This aspect of the job wore him down and he started to realise that he wasn't happy at all with his work.

Having had a passion for fitness for a while now, he realized that he felt very alive when he attended fitness classes and enjoyed working out and teaching others how to work out. He would fiddle with the idea of attending a teacher training course that would allow him to be a professional and certified fitness coach.

As his full time job started to become more of a burden, he became more serious about the prospect of switching careers and pursuing a new one entirely. At his job, realized that the company wasn't generous at all with the incentives and gruelling work hours, but he stayed on as he was afraid he wouldn't find another job in this bad economy. The fear was indeed real so he kept delaying trying to quit his job. Before he knew it 3 years more had passed and by this time he full on dreaded every single minute at his job.

It was not until he made that faithful decision one day to send in his resignation letter and to simultaneously pay for the teacher training course to become a fitness instructor did his fortunes start to change for him. The fortunes in this wasn't about money. It was about freedom. It was about growth. And it was about living.

We all know deep in our hearts when it is time to call it quits to something. When we know that there is nothing more that we can possibly give to our job. That no amount of time more could ever fulfill that void in us. That we just simply need to get out and do something different.

You see, life is about change. As we grow, our priorities change, our personalities change, our expectations change, and our passions and our interests change as well. If we stay in one place too long, especially in a field or in something that we have hit a wall at, we will feel stuck, and we will feel dread. We will feel that our time spent is not productive and we end up feeling hopeless and sorry for ourselves.

Instead when we choose to let go, when we choose to call time on something, we open up the doors for time on other ventures, and other adventures. And our world becomes brighter again.

I challenge each and everyone of you to take a leap of faith. You know deep in your hearts when it is time to move on from your current job and find the next thing. If you dont feel like you are growing, or if you feel that you absolutely hate your job because there is no ounce of joy that you can derive from it, move on immediately. Life is too short to be spending 10 hours of your life a day on something that you hate, that sucks the living soul out of you. Give yourself the time and space to explore, to find some other path for you to take. You will be surprised what might happen when you follow your heart.

I hope you learned something today, take care and I'll see you in the next one.

Chapter 5:

Twenty Percent of Effort Produces

80% of Results

Today we're going to talk about the 80-20 rule and how you can apply it to your life for great results in whatever you are doing. For the purposes of this video we are going to use income as a measurement of success. This will directly translate to productivity and the areas that you are spending your most time and energy.

Have you ever wondered why no matter how much time you end up working, that your paycheck never seems to rise? That your income and finance seems to be stagnant? Or have you ever wondered, for those of you who have ventured into creating a second or third stream of income on the side, that you might actually spend lesser on those activities and earn a bigger income in proportion to the time you actually spent to run those side businesses?

This is where the 80-20 rule comes into play. For those that have not seen their bank account or income grow despite the immense amount of effort put it, It may be that 80% of time you are spending it doing things that actually have little or no change to the growth of your networth. The work simply isn't actually worth 80% of your attention.

Rather you may want to look elsewhere, to that 20%, if you want to see real change. I would recommend that instead of banging your head against the wall at your day job, try looking for something to do on the side. It may be just your passion, or it may be something you foresee greater potential returns. Start taking action on those things. It could be the very thing that you were searching for this whole time. If the rule applies, you should be spending majority of your time and energy into this 20%. By focusing on the tasks that has the greatest rewards, you are working smart instead of working hard now. Only when you can identify what exactly those tasks are can you double down on them for great success.

There were times in my life that I spent a lot of my time trying to force something to work. But no matter how hard I tried, I just couldn't see a breakthrough. It was only after further exploration through trials and errors did I finally come up with a set list of tasks that I knew were profitable. That if I kept doing them over and over again I would be able to grow my wealth consistently. By spending all of my time doing these specific tasks, I was able to eliminate all the noise and to focus my actions to a narrow few. And I was surprised at the outsized rewards it brought me.

If you know that something isn't working, don't be afraid to keep looking, trying, and exploring other ways. Keep a close tab on the time you spend in these areas and the income that flows in. Only when you measure everything can you really know where you are going wrong and where you are going right.

Remember that 20% of the effort produces 80% of the results. So I challenge all of you to stop spending 80% of the effort doing things that only produce 20% of the results. It is better to work smart than to work hard. Trust me. I believe that you will be able to find what those things are if you put your mind to it.

I hope you learned something today, take care and I'll see you in the next one.

Chapter 6:

Wondering If You Have Chosen The Right Career Path

In today's topic we are going to touch on the subject of career once again. Because feeling there's nothing worse than feeling like you are not on the right path, that you are not meant to be where you are right now, that you feel regret for going down this road in the first place.

Hopefully by the end of this video I am able to shed some light into what being on the right career path really means, and that you are indeed on it as we speak.

For those of us who are lucky enough to have gone to get a formal degree in whatever universities in whatever countries, be it IVY league schools, or some neighbourhood universities, we tend to think the course that we have decided to major in will become the thing that we will do for the rest of our lives. But more often than not, for those of us who have had enough work experiences, we know that we don't always end up where we began in our work life.

Life is all about choices and decisions. But life never ever stays the same. When we go out into the real world, sometimes our expectations of a job doesn't match up with reality. And we only realise that after spending enough time pursuing that career path.

From many of my countless interviews and people that I've spoke to, almost all view their degree as a stepping stone to something else. Rarely does one person commit to pursuing their major for the rest of their lives. The only few exceptions being those that go to medical school or some other professional degree that they have invested maybe close to a decade mastering their field of study. The opportunity costs for these people are too high and many a times they stick to their careers because they have already invested too much and are in too deep to back out now.

For the vast majority of us, we tend not to have such a deep and emotional connection to our primary field of study that it is much easier for us to pursue something else if we are not happy. 3 to 4 years while it might sound painful to waste, it certainly doesnt sound as bad as 12 years of education in the medical field. 4 years pre med, 4 years medical school, and then maybe another 4 years residency. All those years truly add up. Not to mention all the school fees that had gone into that.

To answer the question about whether you have pursued the right career path, I believe that you are meant to be exactly where you are right now. Because only when you realise that you may not necessarily like your path, can you actually make the informed decision to do something about it like change job or pursue other fields of interest. Without this experience of the path you are on right now, you just never really know whether you would have regretted not even trying it in the first place.

As humans, it is in our DNA to explore. We love novel experiences, we love to see new things and places, we love to learn and grow. Without all these factors, we may end up feeling like we are actually dying. If we find that our career doesn't give us that satisfaction anymore. Hey It's absolutely okay to feel that way. That gives you the confidence to know that you might want to try something else instead and that maybe this isnt for you. Don't feel like you've wasted time because your skills will most definitely be transferable and another door will open for you should you be brave enough to turn the knob.

With this I challenge each and every one of you to stop asking yourself whether you are on the right career path and start believing that where you are right now is beautiful. That you are meant to be where you are right now and asking the questions that you need to be asking about whether you are happy at your job and if there are other things you might want to consider pursuing. Take the leap of faith and never be afraid to try new things.

I hope you learned something today. Take care and I'll see you in the next one.

Chapter 7:

Why You Are Amazing

When was the last time you told yourself that you were amazing? Was it last week, last month, last year, or maybe not even once in your life?

As humans, we always seek to gain validation from our peers. We wait to see if something that we did recently warranted praise or commendation. Either from our colleagues, our bosses, our friends, or even our families. And when we don't receive those words that we expect them to, we think that we are unworthy, or that our work just wasn't good enough. That we are lousy and under serving of praise.

With social media and the power of the internet, these feelings have been amplified. For those of us that look at the likes on our Instagram posts or stories, or the number of followers on Tiktok, Facebook, or Snapchat, we allow ourselves to be subjected to the validation of external forces in order to qualify our self-worth. Whether these are strangers who don't know you at all, or whoever they might be, their approval seems to matter the most to us rather than the approval we can choose to give ourselves.

We believe that we always have to up our game in order to seek happiness. Everytime we don't get the likes, we let it affect our mood for the rest of the day or even the week.

Have you ever thought of how wonderful it is if you are your best cheerleader in life? If the only validation you needed to seek was from yourself? That you were proud of the work you put out there, even if the world disagrees, because you know that you have put your heart and soul into the project and that there was nothing else you could have done better in that moment when you were producing that thing?

I am here to tell you that you are amazing because only you have the power to choose to love yourself unconditionally. You have the power to tell yourself that you are amazing. and that you have the power to look into yourself and be proud of how far you came in life. To be amazed by the things that you have done up until this point, things that other people might not have seen, acknowledged, or given credit to you for. But you can give that credit to yourself. To pat yourself on the back and say "I did a great job".

I believe that we all have this ability to look inwards. That we don't need external forces to tell us we are amazing because deep down, we already know we are.

If nobody else in the world loves you, know that I do. I love your courage, your bravery, your resilience, your heart, your soul, your commitment, and your dedication to live out your best life on this earth. Tell yourself each and everyday that you deserve to be loved, and that you are loved.

Go through life fiercely knowing that you don't need to seek happiness, validations, and approval from others. That you have it inside you all along and that is all you need to keep going.

Chapter 8:

The Struggle With Time

Today we're going to talk about a topic that isn't commonly looked at in depth. But it is one that we might hopefully find a new appreciation for. And that is TIME.

Time is a funny thing, we are never really aware of it and how much of a limited resource it really is until we get a rude awakening. Most commonly when our mortality is tested. Whether it be a health scare, an accident, a death of a loved one, a death of a pet, we always think we have more time before that. That we will always have time to say i love you, to put off the things we always told ourselves we needed to do, to start making that change, to spend time with the people that mean the most to us.

As we go about our days, weeks and months, being bothered and distracted by petty work, by our bosses, colleagues, trying to climb the corporate ladder, we forget to stop and check in on our fiends and family... We forget that their time may be running out, and that we may not have as much time with them as we think we do, until it is too late, and then we regret not prioritising them first. All the money that we made could not ever buy back the time we have lost with them. And that is something we have to live with if we ever let that happen.

The other funny thing about time is that if we don't set it aside for specific tasks, if we don't schedule anything, we will end up wasting it on something mindless. Whether it be browsing social media endlessly, or bingeing on television, we will never run out of things to fill that time with. Can you imagine that even though time is so precious, we willingly sacrifice and trade it in for self isolation in front of our TVs and computers for hours on end. Sometimes even for days? Or even on mobile games. Some being so addictive that it consumes most of our waking hours if we are not careful.

The Balanced Workaholic

Our devices have become dangerous time wasters. It is a tool Shea its literally sapping the living energy out of us. Which is why some responsible companies have started implementing new features that help us keep track of our screen time. To keep us in check, and to not let our children get sucked into this black hole that we might struggle to climb out of.

I believe the biggest struggle with time that we all have is how to spend it in such a way that we can be happy without feeling guilty. Guilty of not spending it wisely. And I believe the best way to start is to start defining the things that you need to do, and the things that you want to do. And then striking a balance. To set equal amounts of time into each activity so that it doesn't overwhelm or underwhelm you. Spend one hour on each activity each day that you feel will have an impact on your life in a meaningful way, and you can spend your time on television or games without remorse.

So I challenge each of you to make the most of your time. SPending time with loved ones always come first, followed by your goals and dreams, and then leisure activities. Never the other way around. That way you can be at the end of your life knowing that you had not wasted the most precious commodity that we are only given a finite amount of. Money can't buy back your youth, your health, or time with loved ones, so don't waste it.

I believe in each and everyone of you, take care, and as always ill see you in the next one.

Chapter 9:
The Power of Growing 1% Each Day

We all chase growth, we all chase success, but many of us want to be the best overnight, we want to get better 1000% over a month. We expect to lose 50 pounds by the end of the month, so we push ourselves so hard, so fast, so intensely, that we often burn out before the month has even ended.

We apply this same speed to our relationships, our careers, other aspects of our health, and we soon wonder why we cannot sustain this momentum for long.

The reason is that changes must be made gradually. Sure we can go cold turkey by cutting carbs out completely from our diet, but how many of you will agree that by the 4th day, many of us will start bingeing on that big plate of pasta because we just miss it so much.

If instead, we had cut our portions of pasta quota for the week by say 30%, how many of you would agree that it would have been a much better route to take instead of the former?

Today I want to challenge you to totally reframe how you approach change. After you have identified the areas in your life you know you need to work on, I want you to start working on one aspect at a time.

Instead of aiming for a 100% growth and transformation by the end of next week, I want you to tell yourself that you will be a 1% better version of yourself each and every day.

This mindset immediately alleviates any pressure we have on ourselves for drastic changes. Changes that are unsustainable even in the short run. By making incremental changes, we give ourselves the space to grow, to learn, to get better, and to be better.

Take your favourite sport for example. For me it's tennis. I don't expect to become like Federer overnight no matter how hard I believe I can. Instead, i break down each aspect of federer's game and work on fine adjustments to my own game 1% at a time. These 1% gains will compound over time. As with everything else that you do.

If career is an area of focus for you, instead of expecting to become employee of the month by the next month, work instead on becoming a 1% better employee each day. By the end of 100 days, you would've already become more than 100% than you were at the start of your job, and by the end of the year, you would already be so amazing at it that you would've believe how you got there in the first place.

Life is a marathon, not a sprint. If we sprint through life, we will miss all the amazing sights along the way. We will miss the fine details that make the journey worth taking. Similarly, our personal development and growth is also a marathon, not a sprint. We should all keep that in perspective when we approach any new project or endeavour. Only then can we truly make a lasting difference in the areas of our lives that matters to us most.

Chapter 10:

The Problem With Immediate

Gratification

In today's topic we are going to talk about something that I am sure most of us struggle with every single day, myself included. I hope that by the end of this video, you will be able to make better decisions for yourself to maybe think further ahead rather than trying to get gratification right away.

There will be 5 areas that I want to talk about. Finance, social media, shopping, fitness, and career.

Alright if you're ready let's begin.

Let's start with the one thing that i think most of us will find it hard to resist. Shopping. For many of us, buying things can be a form of happiness. When we want something, our dopamine levels rise, and our attention is solely focused on acquiring that object whatever it may be. The anticipation of getting something is something very exciting and our bodies crave that sense of gratification in getting that product. Shopping can also be a form of distraction, maybe from work or from feeling stressed out. Shopping can also arise from boredom and the desire within us to satisfy our cravings for wanting things begins to consume us. This creates a real problem because after we attain the item, often we are not satisfied and start looking for the next thing. This creates a never ending cycle of seeking gratification immediately at the expense of our bank account. And we are soon left with a big hole in the wallet without realising it.

Before I talk about the solutions to this problem, i want to address the other 4 areas on the list.

The next one is social media. We tend to gravitate towards social media apps when we want to fill our time out of most probably boredom. At times when we are supposed to be working, instead of blocking out time to stay focused on the task at hand, we end up clicking on Instagram or Facebook, trying to see if there are any new updates to look at provided to us by the algorithm. Social media companies know this and they exploit our feeble nature with this cheap trick. Everytime we try to refresh a page, we seek immediate gratification. And we create within us a terrible habit hundreds of times a day, checking for updates that wastes hours away from our day.

The next area that maybe isn't so common is in the area of fitness. Instead of laying out a long term plan to improve our health and fitness through regular exercise and choosing healthy foods, we tend to want things happening for us immediately. We think and crave losing 10 pounds by tomorrow and set unrealistic targets that easily lets us down. Hence we seek for quick fix solutions that aim to cut short this process. We may end up trying to take slimming pills, or looking for the next extreme fad or diet to get to our goals quicker. Many of them not ending the right way and can be potentially harmful for our health. For those that cannot control what they eat, in reverse they may seek immediate gratification by bingeing on a fast food meal, ice cream, chocolates, or whatever foods brings them the quickest source of comfort. Many a times at the expense of their weight. All these are also very harmful examples of immediate gratification.

The 4th area I want to talk about is something of bigger importance. And this may not resonate with everybody, but it is about having a career that also focuses on building a side stream of passive income rather than one that focuses on active income. You see active income is static. When we work, we get a pay check at the end of every month. We look forward to that paycheck and that becomes our gratification. But when we stop working, our income stream ceases as well. This desire to keep that paycheck every month keeps us in the jobs that we ate. And we only look towards our jobs as a means to an end, to get that gratification every month in X amounts of dollars. And for many of us who uses shopping as a way to fill the void left by our jobs, we end up using that

Hard earned money to gratify ourselves even more, taking up loans and mortgages to buy more and more things. If this is you, you are definitely not alone.

The final area I want to address in the area of finance. And that goes hand in hand with spending money as well. You see for many of us, we fail to see the power that compounding and time has on our finances. When we spend money today instead of saving or investing it, we lose the potential returns that investments can do for our capital. While it may be fun for us to spend money now to acquire things, it may instead bring us 10x the joy knowing that this $1000 that we have invested could end up becoming $100000 in 30 years when it is time for us to retire. The effects of compounding are astonishing and I urge all of you to take a closer look at investing what you have now as you might be surprised at the amounts of returns you can get in 30-50 years or even sooner.

So where does this lead us in our fight against instant gratification? From the areas we have described, immediate gratification always seem to have a direct negative consequence. When we choose to satisfy our cravings for wanting things fast right now, we feed our inner desires that just keeps craving more. The point is that we will never be satisfied.

If however we take a long-term approach to things and make better decisions to delay our reward, many a times that feeling will return us more than 2 fold than if we had taken it immediately. The problem is that most of us do not possess this sort of patience. Our instinct tells us that now is the best time. But history and the law of life has repeatedly shown us that that is not always true. For many things in our life, things actually gets better with time. The more time you give yourself to heal from a heartbreak, the better it will get. The more time you invest your money, the greater the returns. The more time you spend time on doing something you love, the more happiness you will feel. The more time you put into eating moderately and exercising regularly, the faster you will see your body and health take shape. The more you resist turning on the social media app, the more you will find you won't need its attention after a while. The more time you spend with friends, the deeper the friendship.

The moral of the story in all of this is that giving yourself enough time is the key to success. Trying to get something quick and easy is not always the best solution to everything. You have to put in the time and energy required to see the fruits of your labour. And that is a law that we all have to realise and apply if we want to see true success. Rome isn't built in a day, so why would anything else be? We shouldn't rush through everything that we do expecting fast results and instant gratification.

So i challenge each and everyone of you to take a good look at the areas of your life that you expect fast results and things to happen immediately. See if any of the things that I have mentioned earlier resonates with you and see if you can modify the way you acquire things. I believe that with a little effort, we all can look towards a more rewarding path to success.

Thank you, I hope you learned something today and I'll see you in the next one.

PART 2

Chapter 1:

The 5 Second Rule

Today I'm going to share with you a very special rule in life that has worked wonders for me ever since I discovered it. And that is known as the 5 second rule by Mel Robbins.

You see, on a daily basis, I struggle with motivation and getting things done. I struggle with the littlest things like replying an email, to responding to a work request. This struggle has become such a bad habit that before I think about beginning any sort of work, I would first turn on my Netflix account to watch an episode or two of my favourite sitcom, telling myself that I will get right on it after I satisfy this side of me first.

This habit of procrastination soon became so severe that I would actually sit and end up wasting 4-5 hours of time every morning before I would actually even begin on any work-related stuff. Before I knew it, it would be 3pm and I haven't gotten a single thing done. All the while I was staring at the clock, counting the number of hours I have wasted, while simultaneously addicted to procrastinating that I just could not for the life of me get myself off the couch onto my desk to begin any meaningful work.

I realized that something had to change. If I kept this up, I would not only not get anything done, like ever, but i would also begin to loathe myself for being so incredibly unproductive and useless. This process of self-loathing got worse everyday I leaned into the habit of procrastination. It was only until i stumbled onto Mel Robbin's 5 second rule that I started to see a real change in my habits.

The rule is simple, to count backwards from 5 and to just get up and go do that thing. It sounded stupid to me at first, but it worked. Instead of laying around in bed every morning checking my phone before I woke up, I would count backwards from 5 and as soon as it hit 1, i would get up and head straight towards the shower, or I would pack up my things and get out of my house.

I had identified that staying at home was the one factor that made me the most unproductive person on the planet, and that the only way I knew I was going to get real work done, was to get out of the house. I had also identified that showering was a good way to cleanse my mind from the night before. I really enjoyed showering as I always seem to have a clear head afterwards to be able to focus. What works for me, may not necessarily work for you. You have to identify for yourself when are the times you are most productive, and simply replicate it. A good way to find out is by journaling, which I will talk about in a separate video. Journaling is a good way to capture a moment in time and a particular state of mind. Try it for yourself the next time you are incredibly focused, write down how you got to that state, and simply do it again the next time to get there.

The 5 second rule is so simple yet so powerful because it snaps our unhealthy thought patterns. As Mel puts it, our brain is hardwired to protect us. We procrastinate out of fear of doing the things that are hard, so we have to beat our brain to it by disrupting it first. When we decide to move and take action after reaching 1, it is too late for our brains to stop us. And we get the ball rolling.

I was at my most productive on days that I felt my worst. But I overcame it because I didn't let my brain stop me from myself. I wouldn't say that I am struggle free now, but i knew i had a tool that would work most of the time to get me out of procrastination and into doing some serious work that would move my life forward. There are times when I would forget about the 5 second rule and my bad habits would kick in, but I always reminded myself that it was available to me if I chose to use it.

I would urge all of you who are struggling with any form of procrastination or laziness to give the 5 second rule a try. All you need to do is to get started and the rest becomes easy.

Chapter 2:

Putting Exercise First

In this topic we're going to talk about why you should consider putting exercise first above all else in your daily routine and the benefits that it can bring to your health and all other aspects of your life.

Many of us don't usually prioritise work as the most essential part of our day. We have work, family, kids, money, and a whole host of problems to worry about that exercise usually comes in dead last on the list of things to do. What we fail to realise is that exercise is the one thing that we might need most to keep us fit and healthy to take on the challenges that life throws at us each and every day.

I'm sure you all know the benefits of exercise. Doing it regularly can bring lots of benefits to your metabolism, alertness, energy, BMI, muscle mass, and so on. But what does it really mean?

Have you ever wondered why you are always feeling tired all the time? Or why you feel like you haven't really woken up yet when you're already sitting in front of your desk at the office?

You see, it is the time of your exercise that matters a lot too. A lot of successful CEOs and entrepreneurs actually make exercise the first thing they do when they wake up from bed. The reason is simple, it gets the body moving which in turns starts the engine that drives you out of lethargy and into an active physical state. As you move on a treadmill or do yoga early in the morning, your heart starts pumping faster which drives more blood into other areas of your body to wake you up.

And this sets you up for success because you are no longer in a state of slumber and sluggishness. Exercising first thing in the morning also has the added benefit of checking it off your list early so that you do not wait for the lazy bug to tell you not to enter the gym.

Sure getting up earlier to exercise might also be a struggle in of itself, but you do not necessarily have to travel to a gym far away to get your daily exercise. Simply stepping out of the house for a quick run or finding an empty space in your house where you will not be disturbed and begin a yoga routine that you can find on YouTube will also suffice. As long as you get the body moving and in a state of flow, you would have already won the day.

Putting exercise first above all else in your day also gives you a sense of accomplishment that you have taken the action to improve your health consistently. Losing excess body fat will also increase your energy levels and help you get through the challenges of your work day with greater ease.

If you find that exercising first thing in the morning is just impossible to do for some reason, make it a point to schedule it sometime before midday, preferably during your lunch break. Leaving exercise to the night will only trigger more excuses from your brain not to go as your will power gets depleted more and more throughout the day. From experience, unless I have booked a class that i can't back out of in the evening, more often than not I will find many more excuses not to go than if I had scheduled exercise early in the day.

If there is a sport that you particularly like, I also urge you to schedule more games with friends or family throughout the week as you are more likely to show up for them seeing that you already favour the sport over other exercises. In my case I love tennis and would almost never miss a session that I have scheduled. Gym and yoga on the other hand, I am more inclined to give it a miss if given the opportunity.

So for those of you who want to operate in a higher state of mind, body, and spirit, I challenge you to make exercise your number one priority and put it at the top of your list of things to do for the day. You will find your mind will be clearer and you will know exactly what you need to do for the day as you flow with the exercise. Feel free to play your favourite music playlist as you workout as well.

I hope you learned something today and I'll see you in the next one.

Chapter 3:

Setting Too High Expectations

Today we're going to talk about the topic of setting too high expectations. Expectations about everything from work, to income, to colleagues, friends, partners, children, family. Hopefully by the end of this video I will be able to help you take things down a notch in some areas so that you don't always get disappointed when things don't turn out the way you expect it to.

Let's go one by one in each of these areas and hopefully we can address the points that you are actively engaged in at the moment.

Let's begin with work and career. Many of us have high expectations for how we want our work life to be. How we expect our companies and colleagues to behave and the culture that we are subjected to everyday. More often that not though, companies are in the business of profit-making and cutting costs. And our high expectations may not meet reality and we might end up getting let down. What I would recommend here is that we not set these expectations of our colleagues and bosses, but rather we should focus on how we can best navigate through this obstacle course that is put in front of us. We may want to focus instead on how we can handle ourselves and our workload. If however we find that we just can't shake off this expectations that we want from working in a company, maybe we want to look elsewhere to companies that have a work culture that suits our personality. Maybe one that is more vibrant and encourages freedom of expression.

Another area that we should address is setting high expectations of our partners and children. Remember that we are all human, and that every person is their own person. Your expectations of them may not be their expectations of themselves. When you impose such an ideal on them, it may be hard for them to live up to. Sure you should expect your partner to be there for you and for your children to behave a certain way.

But beyond that everyone has their own personalities and their own thoughts and ideas. And what they want may not be in line with what we want for them. Many a times for Asian parents, we expect our kids to get good grades, get into good colleges, and maybe becoming a doctor or lawyer one day. But how many of us actually understand what our kids really want? How many of us actually listen to what our kids expect of themselves? Maybe they really want to be great at music, or a sport, or even finance. Who's to say what's actually right? We should learn to trust others and let go of some of our own expectations of them and let them become whoever they want to be.

The next area I want to talk about is simply setting too high expectations of yourself. Many times we have an ideal of who we want to be - how we want to look, how we want our bodies to look, and how we want our bank statement to look, amongst many others. The danger here is when we set unrealistic expectations as to when we expect these things to happen. Remember most things in life takes time to happen. The sooner you realise that you need more time to get there, the easier it will be on yourself. When we set unrealistic timelines, while it may seem ideal to rush through the process to get results fast, more often than not we are left disappointed when we don't hit them. We then get discouraged and may even feel like a failure or give up the whole process entirely. Wouldn't it be better if we could give ourselves more time for nature to work its magic? Assuming you follow the steps that you have laid out and the action plans you need to take, just stretch this timeline out a little farther to give yourself more breathing room. If you feel you are not progressing as fast as you had hoped, it is okay to seek help and to tweak your plans as they go along. Don't ever let your high expectations discourage you and always have faith and trust in the process even when it seems hard.

One final thing I want to talk about is how we can shift from setting too high expectations to one of setting far-out goals instead. There is a difference. Set goals that serve to motivate you and inspire you to do things rather than ones that are out of fear. When we say we expect something, we immediately set ourselves up for disappoint. However if we tell ourselves that we really want something, or that we want to achieve something that is of great importance to us, we shift to a goal-oriented mindset. One that is a lot healthier. We no longer fear the deadline creeping up on us. We instead continually work on getting there no matter how long it takes. That we tell ourselves we will get there no matter what, no matter how long. The key is to keep at it consistently and never give up.

Having the desire to work at an Apple store as a retail specialist, I never let myself say that I expect apple to hire me by a certain time otherwise I am never pursuing the job ever again. Rather I tell myself that being an Apple specialist is my dream job and that I will keep applying and trying and constantly trying to improve myself until Apple has no choice but to hire me one day. A deadline no longer bothers me anymore. While I wait for them to take me in, I will continue to pursue other areas of interest that will also move my life forward rather than letting circumstances dictate my actions. I know that I am always in control of my own ship and that I will get whatever I put my mind to eventually if I try hard enough.

So with that I challenge each and every one of you to be nicer to yourselves. Lower your lofty expectations and focus on the journey instead of the deadline. Learn to appreciate the little things around you and not let your ego get in the way.

I hope you learned something today, take care and I'll see you in the next one.

Chapter 4:

Put Yourself In Positions of

Opportunity

Today I examined a story of a very famous woman in Singapore who had a less than perfect childhood, but grew up to become a big personality in the media industry. The woman I am fascinated today is the artiste known as Sharon Au.

You see, Sharon was a child of divorced parents. She moved from home to home, staying with relatives up until she was 17. Her parents were never really there for her but she had something special in her. She was resilient and she always strived to be the best.

While she did not intend to be a famous personality, she auditioned for a role as a dancer in a musical after having seen it many times before on stage, learning the songs word for word. This immediately impressed the auditioner who casted her the role of the lead.

Now we have our first example of how she had placed herself in a position of opportunity and got herself a start in what would be a lucrative career as a media personnel. The first takeaway is that she dared to try. She dared to audition. And she dared to challenge herself to be placed in a role where she could further showcase her talents. This was her at age 20.

With this first opened door, she and her cast in the musical managed to sell out 16 shows. And as luck would have it once again, she made a remarkable performance on one of the show nights while a big head of a media executive company was there to watch. She was offered a contract immediately and from there her media career took off.

She subsequently appeared in countless tv shows and became a prominent tv personality in the Singapore media industry. As her fame and popularity escalated, so did the number of opportunities in the form of contracts and endorsements that followed. She subsequently became so popular that she won numerous awards and accolades for her performance as a host and actress.

After spending more than 10 years in the media industry, she decided to pursue her initial dream of going to university at age 30. She left her lucrative entertainment career in Singapore for a university in Japan and appeared on the deans list multiple times while impressively studying and completing her education in a foreign language. She is now currently a investment director working in Paris.

I just want to impress on you today on how one decision in her life, to audition for a role in a musical, let to a chain of events that brought her much successes in her very fulfilling yet ever changing career in work and life. She had effectively placed herself in a position of opportunity one time which had led to multiple opportunities and doors opening for her like a floodgate. Barring her talent and tireless work ethic that should inspire everyone should you dig deeper into her life and career, she remains a gem in Singapore's history as an icon who had left a mark on the entertainment history even till this day.

I want to challenge all of you to not give up in placing yourself in areas where opportunities can present themselves to you. You might not know when or how it might hit you, but when it does, it can come so fast and so great that you better be prepared for it.

I hope you all enjoyed the sharing today and i hope you learned something new to improve your life and situation. As always see you in the next one.

Chapter 5:

Make Friends With Your Problems

Today we're going to talk about a topic that I hope will inspire you to view your problems not as a hurdle to your goals, but a necessity. How you can make friends with your problems to eventually see it as a part of your journey towards greater success.

You see, problems arise in all aspects of our lives every single day. As we go through life, we start to realise that life is merely about problem solving. When we are growing up, we face the problems of not being able to stand on our own two feet, problems about not being able to potty train, problems with peeing in the bed, problems with riding a new bicycle, problems with school, problems with Teachers, problems with our homework.

But the thing is that as kids, we view these problems as challenges. As something to work towards. We don't necessarily view problems as a negative thing, and we always strive to overcome these problems, never giving up until we do so. And through this perseverance, we grow and evolve. But as we get older, and our child-like response to problems start to change, we start seeing problems in a different way. Problems become obstacles rather than challenges, and problems sometimes overwhelm us to the point where we are not able to function.

We face problems in getting into good high schools and universities, problems in getting a job, problems with family, problems with relationships, problems with bosses, problems with colleagues, problems with starting a family. All these are legitimate problems that I am very sure every single one of us will face at some point in our lives. And the problems will never stop coming.

From what I have shared so far, it is very clear that problems are a way of life, and problems will never go away. A life without problems is really not life at all.

Personally, I have dealt with my fair share of problems. I struggled greatly with getting good grades in university, I struggled in serving for the army as part of mandatory conscription for my country, I struggled with pressures from work, and these problems at times got to me where I felt that I could not see the light at the end of the tunnel. These problems consumed my vision that I could not see the big picture. That life is beautiful, and that my problems are nothing compared to what life has to offer.

In that moment as I was living through those problems however, I could not see the light. I was laser focused on the problem at hand and at many stages, I did feel depressed. I felt unworthy. I felt like I couldn't handle my problems.

I am not sure if my inability to handle problems as I grew older were genetic, or that my character just wasn't strong enough to withstand pressures from the external world. But I did feel like it became harder and harder each year.

What I failed to realise, and that goes back to how I saw problems when I was young, was that I viewed my problems as an enemy rather than a friend. I saw my problems as something that was getting in the way of my goals, rather than a necessary part of the process towards that goal.

By the time I was 20, I wanted a life without problems. I didn't want to deal with any more problems anymore. And as unrealistic as that sounded, I actually believed that it was what I wanted. And every problem that came my way felt like a mountain. A major annoyance that would take every ounce of my energy to overcome. And that negative view to problems actually made my life much more miserable.

It was only in my late twenties that I saw more of life did my perception of problems start to shift profoundly. I learned of the struggles that my parents had to go through to get the life that I was living today, I saw in many of my peers that work life is actually tough and those that viewed their job negatively almost always ended up depressed and unworthy while those that saw their work as challenges actually grew as people.

That shift happened gradually but I started to see the problems that came up in my daily life as friends rather than as enemies. I started to view the mandatory things I had to do to sustain myself financially, emotionally, physically, as simply a way of life. In areas such as health and fitness where I tend to struggle with a lot, which was quite a big problem in my opinion, i simply found alternative ways to keep fit that worked for me rather than get obsessed with the way i looked.

In areas of finance and career, where I also saw as a big problem, I adapted by adopting a completely novel way of working that actually made my work much more meaningful and enjoyable instead of subscribing myself to a job that I know that I would hate.

I started to view each problem as challenges again that would require my knowledge and expertise to overcome. And it started to consume me less and less. I made them my friends instead of my enemy. And when one door closes, I was always resourceful to find another open door to get me to where I wanted to go.

So I challenge each and everyone of you to start seeing your problems not as hindrances to your goals, but as challenges that requires your smartness to conquer. I believe that you have the power to knock down every problem that comes your way no matter how great the challenge is. However if it does become overwhelming, it is okay to walk away from it. Don't let it consume you and don't obsess over a problem until it wrecks your health mentally and physically. Life is too short for problems to ruin us. If it can't be made friends with, it is okay to simply let it go. Nothing good can come from sheer force.

I hope you have learned something today, and as always take care and I'll see you in the next one.

Chapter 6:

Overcoming Tiredness and

Lethargy

Tiredness and lethargy has become a major problem for youths and adults these days. As our lives get busier and our ability to control our sleep gets more out of hand, we all face a constant struggle to stay alert and engaged in our life's work every single day. And this problem hits me as well.

You see, many of us have bad sleep habits, and while it might feel good to stay up late every night to watch Netflix and binge on YouTube and Instagram posts, we pay for it the next day by being a few hours short of a restful night when our alarm wakes us up abruptly every morning.

We tell ourselves that not needing so much sleep is fine for us, but our body tells us a different story. And we can only fake being energetic and awake for so long. Sooner or later we will no doubt experience the inability to function on an optimal level and our productivity and mood will also be affected accordingly. And this would also lead to overall tiredness and lethargy in the long run.

Before we talk about what we can do to counter and fix this problem that we have created for ourselves, we first have to understand why we consciously allow ourselves to become this tired in the first place.

I believe that many of us choose entertainment over sleep every night is because we are in some ways or another overworked to the point that we don't have enough time to ourselves every single day that we choose to sacrifice our sleep time in order to gain back that few hours of quality personal time. After spending a good 10 hours at our jobs from 9-6pm, and after settling down from the commute home and factoring in dinner time, we find ourselves with only a solid 1-2 hours of time to watch our favourite Netflix shows or YouTube, which i believe is not very much time for the average person.

When presented with the choice of sleep versus another episode or two of our guilty pleasure, it becomes painfully obvious which is the "better" choice for us. And we either knowingly or unknowingly choose entertainment and distraction over health.

Basically, I believe the amount of sleep you choose to give yourself is directly proportionate to how happy you are about your job. Because if you can't wait to get up each and everyday to begin your life's work, you will give yourself the best possible sleep you can each night to make sure you are all fired up the next day to crush your work. But conversely, if you hate your job and you feel like you have wasted all your time at work all day, you will ultimately feel that you will need to claim that time back at night to keep yourself sane and to keep yourself in the job no matter how much you dislike it. Even if it means sacrificing precious sleep to get there.

So I believe the real question is not how can we force ourselves to sleep earlier every night to get the 8 hours of sleep that we need in order not to feel tired and lethargic, but rather is there anything we can change about how we view our job and work that we come home at the end of the day feeling recharged and fulfilled to the extend that we don't have to look for a way to escape every night into the world of entertainment just to fill our hearts.

When you have found something you love to do each day, you will have no trouble going to bed at 10pm each night instead of 1 or 2am.

So I challenge each and everyone of you to take a hard look at WHY you are not getting enough sleep. There is a high chance that it could boil down to the reason I have described here today, and maybe a change in careers might be something to consider. But if you believe that this tiredness and lethargy is born out of something medical and genetic, then please do go see a doctor to get a medical solution to it.

Otherwise, take care and I wish you all the best in reclaiming back your energy to perform at your peak levels of success. See you in the next one.

Chapter 7:

Overcoming Your Fears

Today we're going to talk about the topic of fears. What fear is and how we can overcome it. Now before we dive into it, let us just take a brief moment to think of or right down what our greatest fears are right now.

Whether it be taking the next step in your relationship, fear of the unknown, fear of quitting your job and not finding another one, fear or death, fear of illnesses, whatever fear that jumps out at you and is just eating at you at the back of your mind, i want you to remember that fear as we go through this video.

So what is fear exactly? Whilst there are many definitions of fear out there, I'm going to take, as usual, my spin on things. And to me fear is simply a negative feeling that you assign to usually a task that you really don't want to do. And most of the time, the fear is of the unknown, that you can't visualise what is going to happen next. You don't know whether the outcome will be good or bad, and you don't know whether it is the right move to make. So this trio of thoughts keep circling round and round and eventually you just decide that you are not going to take any action on it and you just shove it to one side hoping that it goes away. And whilst you may do that temporarily, sometimes even for months, one day you are going to have to come face to face with it again. And when that day comes, you will either be paralysed again or you may again put it off to a later date.

We procrastinate on our fears because we want a sure thing. We want to know what will happen next, and we fear what we don't know.

Now for the fears that we are talking about today, it is something that will affect your life if u don't take action. If it is like a fear of bungee jumping or sky driving, sure that fear is physical and very real, but also you can make a choice not to do it and your problem is solved. It will not affect your life in a negative way if u don't do it.

But if it is a fear of a career switch because you already hate your job so much and are totally miserable, that is a fear that you should do your best to try and address as soon as possible.

So what can and should you do about these sorts of fears? The answer for this one is not going to be that difficult. Simply think of the consequences of not conquering your task and how much it might prevent you from moving forward in life and you have got your answer.

When the pain associated with not accomplishing the task becomes greater than the fear we assign to it, it is the tipping point that we need to finally take that action. But instead of waiting to get to that excruciating pain, we can visualise and project what it could potentially feel like if we don't do it now and the pain we might feel at a later day, say 1 year from now, when we have wasted another full year of our life not taking that leap of faith, the time we have burned, the time we can never get back, and the opportunity cost of not taking action now, we might just decide that we don;t want to wait until that day comes and face that huge amount of regret that we should've done something a lot sooner.

And what we need to simply do is to just take action. Taking action is something you will hear from all the gurus you will find out there. When faced with a fear or challenge, instead of wondering what dangers lurk in the unknown, just take action and let the experience tell you whether it was indeed the right or wrong decision. Do you necessary homework and due diligence beforehand and take that calculated step forward instead of procrastinating on it. Life is too short to be mucking around. Just go for it and never live your life in fear or regret ever again.

I challenge each and everyone of you to go through the list that we have created at the start of the video. The one that you have been most fearful of doing. And i want you to assess the pros and cons of each fear that you have written down. If there are more pros than cons, i want you to set a deadline for yourself that you will take action on it. And that deadline is today. Don't waste precious time worrying and instead spend more time doing.

I hope you learned something today and as always take care and i wish you all the best in overcoming your fears and achieving your goals as fast as possible. See you in the next one.

Chapter 8:

How To Take Action

Today we're going to talk about something pretty crucial. And this also plays into the topics of motivation, purpose, and goals. And that is, "How To Take Action". Before we begin, i want you to write down a couple of things that you were supposed to take action on but have been putting it off for whatever reason. And i want you to keep these things in mind as we go through this video. And hopefully by the end of it, i would have been able to convince you to take action and to start moving forward in your bigger life projects as well.

Why is Taking Action so important? To put it simply, taking action is the one thing that we can control to move us towards our goals. Whether we succeed or not is irrelevant in this case. Many of us hesitate to take action because we are afraid of failure. We fear the unknown and we over analyse and over think things to a point that we become paralysed. And I'm sure you guys have heard this term before: and that is analysis paralysis.

We draw up such detailed plans for how to are going to tackle this problem, we tweak and tweak the draft, aiming to find perfection before we even take the first action step to begin doing the work. And many times, for many people, we just let the plan sit on the shelves or in our computer, afraid to take action because we fear that we might not be able to accomplish the goal we have set out for ourselves.

You see, planning and drafting isn't going to move the needle. When we have a project, planning only makes up a small part of the process. And completion of the project is always down to every member of the group taking action and completing their part of the task. Or in the case of a solo project, all of the action and effort put in comes from you.

When we plan for anything, even for our future, it is something that keeps us in check, to have a reference for us to know that we are on the right track. But whether or not we follow those plans are entirely up to the actions that we actually take. Whether we do save that $100 every month, or not spend money on unnecessary things, or say that we are going to invest in constant education and growth, these are not set in stone if we do not take action.

Another thing that holds us back from taking action is the fear that we will make mistakes. And that we will feel like a fool if we did things wrongly. But if you look at your life, realistically, how many times have you actually done something right the first time around on something that you haven't actually tried before? For example riding a bike, swimming, learning a new language, learning a new instrument. Wouldn't you agree that making mistakes is actually part of the process? Without practice there's not perfect, so why do we think that we will always get it right the first time when it comes to starting a new business or taking action on whatever new thing that we had set our sights on?

We have no problem telling ourselves that making mistakes in smaller things is okay but we berate ourselves or we create this immense expectation that we must get things right the first time around on bigger projects that we fear the climb because we fear the thought of falling down. And we don't even give ourselves a chance to prove that we can do it.

To counter this, we must tell ourselves that making mistakes is a part of the process, to not rush the process, and to give ourselves more room for failure so that we will have the best chance of actually succeeding someday. However long it takes. We must trust the process because it will happen for us eventually. The only time we really do fail is the last time we actually stop trying, stop taking action, and stop learning from our mistakes. that is the time when we can say we are a failure, if we quit. But if we never give up, and we keep taking action, it will work out for us.

One final hurdle that many of us face is that we tend to want to rush the process and we set unrealistic deadlines to achieve those goals. If we go back to our previous example of learning a new instrument, how many of you guys will agree that, although not impossible, it is unrealistic to become a guitar guru after the 1st year? Most of us would realistically say that it will take at least a few years of daily practice to actually become a pro guitar player. But how many of us actually apply that same concept to a big project like growing our income from $3k to $10k. We all expect fast results and fast growth, but rarely does things work out so smoothly, unless we are incredibly lucky.

When we set these big targets but fail to realise that we need to take baby steps consistently everyday, we set ourselves up for failure without realising it. Without giving ourselves the room to grow a seed into a tree, we end up chopping it down when it is still at the early growth stages. And we fail to let time and effort do it's thing, giving it water and light day in and day out. And we beat ourselves up when we quit prematurely.

What I have learnt, from experience, is that the best way to achieve something eventually, is to take baby steps, taking a little action each day, be it 5 mins, an hour, or 10 hours, they all count. And instead of just hoping to rush to the end, that I actually learned to not only enjoy the process, but also to trust that my efforts will all pay off in the end. And many a times, they did. I left the fear and worry to one side and just focused on taking action. I stopped comparing myself with my peers, and focused on my own journey. I can't control how much faster my competition can grow or achieve, but i can definitely control my own destiny.

So i challenge each and everyone of you today to take a look at the list of things that you hope to achieve that you have written down at the start of this video, and to take the first step of stop trying to perfect the plan, to stop thinking and worrying about what might and could go wrong, to stop fearing the unknown, and to simply just take a little action each day. The worse thing that you can do to yourself is to not even try. You will make mistakes along the way, but as long as you learn from them, you will be moving in the right direction.

I hope you guys learned something today and I hope you work hard towards your dreams. Take care and I'll see you in the next one.

Chapter 9:

How To Stop Procrastinating

Procrastination; perhaps the most used word of our generation. Procrastination can range from a minor issue that hurts your productivity or a significant issue that's preventing you from achieving your goals. You feel powerless, and you feel hopeless; you feel de-motivated, De-strategized, even guilty and ashamed, but all in vain.

Let me in all of you on a secret of life, the need to avoid pain and the desire to gain pleasure. That is what we consider the two driving forces of life. Repeat this mantra till it gets in the back of your head. And if you don't take control over these two forces, they'll take control over you and your entire life. The need to avoid pain is what gets us into procrastinating. We aren't willing to step out of our comfort zone, be uncomfortable, fear the pain of spending our energies, fear failure, embarrassment, and rejection. We don't simply procrastinate because there's no other choice; we procrastinate because whatever it is, we don't consider it essential to us. It's not that something meaningful for us or urgent to us, and when something doesn't feel binding to us, we tend to put it off. We link to link a lot of pain to not taking action. But what if we reversed the roles? What if we start to connect not taking action to be more painful than taking action. We have to change our perspective. See that the long-term losses of not taking action are 1000x more painful than the short-term losses of taking those actions.

Stop focusing on the short-term pain of spending your time, energy, and emotions on the tasks at hand. START focusing on the long-term pain that comes when you'll realize you're not even close to the goals you were meant to achieve.

Stop your desire to gain pleasure from the unnecessary and unimportant stuff. You would rather skip your workout to watch a movie instead. You're focusing on the pleasure, the meaningless short-term craving that'll do you no good. Imagine the pleasure we'd gain if we actually did that workout. Stop making excuses for procrastinating. Start owning up to yourself, your tasks, your goals. Set a purpose in your life and start working tirelessly towards it. Take breaks but don't lose your focus!

If you're in school and you're not getting the grades that you want, and still you're not doing anything about it, then maybe it's not a priority for you. But how do we make it meaningful? How do we make it purposeful? You need to find that motivation to get yourself going. And I promise you once you find that purpose, you'll get up early in the morning, and you'll start working to make your dreams come true.

Don't just talk about it, be about it! You were willing to graduate this year, you were willing to go to the gym and change your physique, you were willing to write that book, but what happened? You didn't make them a priority, and you eventually got tired of talking. Take a deep breath and allow yourself to make the last excuse there is that's stopping you from whatever it is that you're supposed to do. I don't have enough money; I don't write well, I don't sing well, I don't have enough knowledge, that's it. That's the last excuse you're going to make and get it over with. Aren't you tired of feeling defeated? Aren't you tired of getting beat? Aren't you tired of saying "I'll get it done soon" over and over again? To all the procrastinators, YOU. STILL. HAVE. PLENTY. OF. TIME. Don't quit, don't give up, don't just lay there doing nothing; you can make it happen. But not with that procrastinating. Set up a goal, tear it into manageable pieces, stop talking about the things you were going to do, and start doing them for real!

It's not too late for anything. There might be some signs that'll show you that you need to rest. Take them. Take the time you need to get back on track. But don't give up on the immediate gratification. Don't listen to that little voice in your head. Get out of bed, lift those weights, start working on that project, climb that mountain. You're the only person that's stopping you from achieving your goals, your dreams. With long-term success, either you're going to kick the hell out of life, or life's going to kick the hell out of you; whichever of that happens the most will become your reality. We're the master of our fates, the ambassador of our ambitions; why waste our time and lives away into doing something that won't even matter to us in a few years? Why not work towards something that will touch people, inspire them, give them hope.

I'll do it in the next hour, I'll do it the next day, I'll do it the next week, and before you know, you're dragging it to the next month or even next year. And that's the pain of life punching you in the face. The regrets of missing opportunities will eventually catch up to you. Every day you get a chance to either make the most out of life or sit on the sidelines taking the crumbles which people are leaving behind. Take what you want or settle for what's left! That's your choice.

You have to push yourself long past the point of boredom. Boredom is your worst enemy. It kills more people in the pursuit of success than anything or anyone will ever destroy. Your life just doesn't stop accidentally. It's a series of actions that you either initiate or don't initiate. Some people have already made their big decisions today, after waking up. While some, they're still dwelling on the things that don't matter. They're afraid of self-evaluation, thus wasting their time. So focus on yourself, focus on what you're doing with your time, have clarity on what you're trying to achieve. Build into what you're trying to accomplish. Between where you are and where you want to go, there's a skill set that you have to master. There's a gap that's asking for your hard work. So pay the price for what you want to become.

Chapter 10:

Learning To Trust Others

Today we're going to talk about a topic that has the potential to make or break your working relationships or personal relationships with others.

Trust is something that consistently ranks on the top of relationship goals and it has very good reasons for that. Without trust there is basically no foundation. When you can't trust someone, it basically means that you don't believe they can be left alone without your supervision. If you don't trust someone to do the work you have passed along to them, basically it means you are either micro-managing them all day long or that you might just end up doing the work entirely yourself because you don't believe that they can do a job up to your expectations. How many of you have experienced bosses who are micro-managers like that? Basically it either means that they think they can do a better job or that they don't trust you to do the work at all. And we all hate bosses who are like that. Look into mirror like that now, are you doing that to someone at your workplace now?

If you don't trust someone in a relationship, basically you don't believe that they can't be left to their own devices either if they are out of your sight. You start to worry about what they might do when you're gone. If a partner has cheated on you before, I bet that trust has probably gone out the window and it might take a lot of time and energy to actually start trusting that person again. If you don't trust a friend, you might not want to tell them secrets for fear that they may go round sharing it with others without your consent. That plays into the concept of trustworthiness as well. It all comes in a package.

To build trust, we have to earn it. With our actions we can show others that we can be trusted with information, secrets, work, to be faithful, and to do right thing at all times. But trust works both ways as well. If we want people to trust us, we must be willing to extend the trust to others as well. If others have displayed level of competency, we need to start learning to trust that they can get the work done without breathing down their necks all times of the day. If however they come back with shoddy work, maybe you might want to keep a closer eye on them before you feel that their work is up to your standards.

Let others prove to you otherwise by giving them the benefit of the doubt first and then assessing their abilities after.

When you show others that you trust them to do a task, more often than not they will feel a sense of urgency and responsibility to get the work done properly and promptly so that they can show you that they are capable. To show you that they are competent and worthy of the trust that you have placed in them. When you can learn to trust can you truly let go and live life freely. Always having to micro-manage others can not only hurt your reputation as "that guy" but also allow you to have more time do focus on areas where your attention is really required. When you can learn to trust can you truly expand and grow a team, business, company, friendships, and relationships.

I challenge each and everyone of you to learn to trust others and not feel like you have to manage everyone around you to the granular level. If you feel that you have trust issues, for whatever reason, consider working on it or maybe even seeking help. Trust issues usually stems from a past traumatic event or experience that may have impacted your ability to trust again. If so you may one to dig deeper to discover the root of the problem and work through it till the feeling goes away.

Take care and I'll see you in the next one.

6 Ways On How To Change Your Body Language To Attract Success

"If you want to find the truth, do not listen to the words coming to you. Rather see the body language of the speaker. It speaks the facts not audible." - Bhavesh Chhatbar.

Our body language is exceptionally essential as 60-90% of our communication with others is nonverbal. If properly used, it can be our key to more tremendous success. We focus more on our business plans, our marketing drives, and our spreadsheets rather than considering our facial expressions, posture, or what our physical gestures might be saying about us. Our mindset also plays a role in how our body language expresses itself. No matter how impressive our words maybe, if we are sending a negative signal with our body language, we would eventually lose the opportunities of gaining more success.

Here is a list to help you change your body language to attract more success.

1. The Power of Voice

Your personal voice has a huge impact and can literally make or break your success. It is one of the most direct routes to empower your communication. The pitch of your voice, its timbre, cadence, volume, and the speed with which you speak, are all influential factors that will ensure how convincing you are and how people will judge your character.

Lowering your voice at the right moment or injecting some spontaneity into it when needed will enhance your credibility and lend you an air of intelligence. We must fill our voices with our range and depth if we want others and ourselves to take us seriously.

2. The Power of Listening

An excellent speaking skill represents only half of the leadership expression. The other half is mastering your art in listening. While a good listener is incredibly rare, it is essential to keep our ears open to any valuable information that is often silently transmitted. When we start listening attentively to others, we begin to notice what a person is saying and decode accurately what they don't say. You will also begin to realize what the other person is thinking or whether their attitude is positive or hostile towards you. With these particular observations, you will likely attune to another person and create the bond crucial to a successful working life.

3. The Necessity for Emotional Intelligence

The skill of acute listening develops our emotional intelligence, the intuition to ascertain the objective reality of the situation. When we lack emotional intelligence, we might misinterpret situations and fail to decipher what might be needed. Emotional intelligence deepens our empathy. It gives us the ability to be present and listen to someone when they need it the most. It is the single best predictor of performance in the workplace and can be the most vital driver of personal excellence and leadership. Our understanding of emotional intelligence will vastly improve our internal relations and can also deepen our sense of personal fulfillment and professional accomplishment.

4. The Power of Eye Contact

Making eye contact and holding it is seen as a sign of confidence, and the other person is felt valued. It increases your chance of being trustful and respected as they tend to listen to you more attentively and feel comfortable giving you their insights. You may be shy, an introvert, or might have heard that it's impolite to maintain eye contact with a superior. But in many parts of the world, business people expect you to maintain eye contact 50-60% of the time. Here's a simple tip: when you meet someone, look into their eyes long enough to notice their eye color.

5. Talk With Your Hands

There's a region in our brain called the Broca's area, which is essential and active during our speech production and when we wave our hands. Gestures are integrally linked to speech, so gesturing while talking can speed up your thinking. Using hand gestures while talking can improve verbal content as well as make your speechless hesitant. You will see that it will help you form clearer thoughts with more declarative language and speak in tighter sentences.

6. Strike A Power Pose

Research conducted at Harvard and Columbia Business Schools into the effects of body posture and confidence show that holding your body in expansive high-power poses (such as leaning back with hands behind the head or standing with legs and arms stretched wide open) for only as little as two minutes can stimulate high levels of testosterone (a hormone linked to power) and lower levels of cortisol (a stress hormone). You will look and feel more confident and inevitable, leading to an increased feeling of energy and a high tolerance for risk.

Conclusion

Most of our body language and movement are subconscious, so it can be challenging to retrain ourselves away from habits we have had for years. Still, we must try to master our body language, too, with the art of public speaking. Regular practice Is the key to success and the quickest route to attain confident body language as with any other skill. Practice them in your day-to-day life so that they may become deep-rooted. Be less compliant and step into an edgier, emboldened, and more genuine you.

PART 3

Chapter 1:

Share Your Troubles Freely and Openly

Life is hard. We go through tons of challenges, problems, and obstacles every single day. We accumulate problems and stresses left right and Center. Absorbing each impact blow for blow.

Over time, these impacts will wear us down mentally and physically. Without a proper release channel, we find that our emotions spill over in ways when we least expect it. We get easily irritated, have a hard time falling asleep, have mood issues, and find ourselves even being temporarily depressed at times.

When we bottle negativity, it festers inside us without us realising what we have done. That is where releasing those tensions by pouring our heart and soul into friends, writing, journaling, and other outlets that allow us to express our feelings freely without judgement.

We may not all have friends that we can truly count on to share our deepest darkest secrets for fear that they might share these secrets unsuspectingly. If we do have these types of friends, treasure them and seek them out regularly to share your problems. By bouncing ideas off someone, we may even find a new solution to an old problem that we couldn't before. The other party may also be able to see things more objectively and with a unique perspective that is contrary to yours which you could potentially use to your advantage.

If writing things down is something that helps you cope with life, then by all means take a piece of paper and write down all the things that have been bothering you.

Journal it, archive it. You may even write a song about it if that helps you process things better. Writing things down help us clear our minds and lets us see the big picture when we come back to it at a later date should we feel ready to address it. When things are too crazy, we may not have the mental capacity to handle everything being thrown at us at one go. So take the time to sort those feelings out.

You may also choose to just find a place that brings you relaxation. Whether it be going to the beach, or renting a hotel, or even just screaming at the top of your lungs. Let those feelings out. Don't keep it hidden inside.

IF all these things still don't work for you, you may want to try seeking help from a professional counsellor or therapist who can work out these issues you have in your life one by one. Never be afraid to book an appointment because your mental health is more important than the stigma associated with seeing a professional. You are not admitting you have a problem, you are simply acknowledge that there are areas in your life that you need assistance with. And that it is perfectly okay and perfectly normal to do so. Counsellors have the passion to serve, the passion to help, and that is why they chose that profession to being with. So seek their assistance and guidance as much as you need to.

Life isn't easy. But we can all take a conscious effort to regulate our emotions more healthily to live a long and balanced life.

Chapter 2:

Playing To Your Strengths

Have you ever asked yourself why you fail at everything you touch?

Why you seem to lack behind everyone you strive to beat?

Why you can't give up the things that are keeping you from achieving the goals you dream?

Has anyone told you the reason for all this?

You might wonder about it all your life and might never get to the right answer. Even though you stare at the answer every day in the mirror.

Yes! It's you! You are the reason for your failures.

You are the reason for everything bad going on in your life right now.

But you are also the master of your life, and you should start acting like one.

When the world brings you down, find another way to overcome the pressures.

Find another way to beat the odds.

Adverse situations only serve to challenge you.

Be mentally strong and bring the world to your own game.

Show the world what you are.

Show the world what you are capable of.

Don't let anyone dictate to you what you should do.

Rather shape your life to dictate the outcome with your efforts and skills.

You can't always be wrong.

Somewhere, and somehow, you will get the right answer.

That will be your moment to build what you lost.

That will be your moment to shut everyone else and rise high in the silence of your opponents.

If you don't get that chance, don't wait for it to come.

Keep going your way and keep doing the things you do best.

Paths will open to your efforts one day.

You can't be bad at everything you do.

You must be good at something.

Find out what works for you.

Find out what drives your spirit.

Find out what you can do naturally while being blind-folded with your hands tied behind your back.

There is something out there that is calling out to you.

Once you find it, be the best at it as you can.

It doesn't matter if you do not get to the top.

You don't anything to prove to anyone.

You only need one glimpse of positivity to show yourself that you have something worthwhile to live for.

Always challenge yourself.

If you did 5 hours of work today, do 7 tomorrow.

If you run 1 mile today, hit 3 by the end of the week.

You know exactly what you are capable of.

Play to your strengths.

Make it your motto to keep going every single day.

Make a decision.

Be decisive.

Stick with it.

Don't be afraid because there is nothing to fear.

The only thing to fear is the fear itself.

Tell your heart and your mind today, that you can't stop, and you won't stop.

Till the time you have the last breath in your lungs and the last beat in your heart, keep going.

You will need to put your heart out to every chance you can get to raise yourself from all this world and be invincible.

You have no other option but to keep going.

To keep trying until you have broken all the barriers to freedom.

You are unique and you know it.

You just need to have the guts to admit that you are special and live up to the person you were always meant to be.

Take stock of yourself today.

Where are you right now and where do you want to be?

The moment you realize your true goal, that is the moment you have unlocked your strengths.

Live your life on your terms.

Every dream that you dream is obtainable.

And the only way is to believe in yourself.

To believe that you are the only thing standing in the way of your past and your future.

Once you have started, tell yourself that there is no return.

Dictate your body to give up only when you have crossed the finish line.

Start acting on every whim that might get you to the ultimate fate.

These whims are your strength because you have them for a purpose.

Why walk when you can run?

Why run when you can fly?

Why listen when you can sing?

Why go out and dine when you can cook?

The biggest gift that you can give to yourself is the mental satisfaction that you provide yourself.

You are only limited to the extent you cage yourself.

The time you let go will be your salvation. But you have to let go!

Chapter 3:

Pressures of Social Media

Ah social media. This piece of technology has he power to either make us better people and more connected, or wreck us all completely. I want to address this topic today because I feel that social media is a tool that has uses that can impact us either negatively or positively, depending on how we use it. For the purpose of this video, we will talk about how social media can affect our self-worth and self-esteem.

For most of us, when we first hop onto social media, our goal is to connect with our friends. We hop onto Facebook and Instagram to add our friends and to see what's up in their lives, and to be involved with them digitally so to speak. We start by chatting them up and checking out their photos and posts. And we feel happy to be part of a bigger network.

However sooner or later, we get sucked into the pressure of acquiring more people to boost our profile... to get more likes... to get more followers... to become... famous. And every time we post something, we always feel inferior that we don't have as many likes as our friends. That we are somehow unpopular. Furthermore, we start comparing our lives with our friends, and we see what a wonderful life they have lived, the amazing photos that they have taken around the world, and we start wondering where we had gone wrong in our lives, and why we are in such a "terrible" state. We start to wonder if we had made a mistake in our career paths and we constantly compare ourselves to others that make ourselves feel Low.

Another pressure we face from social media is in the area of body image and self-worth. We see posts of the world of the insta-famous, their chiseled bodies, their chiseled faces, their amazing hair, amazingly toned skin and beauty standards that we just can't help but compare ourselves to. We start feeling inferior and we start to think we are not beautiful. We then look for ways to improve the way we look that always makes us feel so lousy about ourselves. What's more is that we come across posts of people with amazing houses and with money beyond our wildest imaginations and we again beat ourselves up for it. We wonder why we are not in that same place in life as them.

Every time we open the app to see these accounts, this regular and constant comparisons leaves us with terrible Low self-esteem and self-worth that manifests in us day in and day out. And over time, it becomes part of our negative outlook on our own lives.

I had subjected myself to a few of these before when I first started out on social media. It became all too easy to bow to the pressure of social media when all you are feeding your mind every single day is the same exactly self-harming thing.

It was only after I took a break from social media and had time to grow up a little bit that I started to use social media in a much healthier way.

After coming back to social media after a long hiatus, I stopped chasing likes, stop chasing new followers, and focused on merely reconnecting once again with my friends. I stopped browsing random accounts that will always get me lost in this rabbit hole and I felt much better about myself. As I grew up, I stopped comparing myself to others but rather view people who are in better places than I was as ways to inspire me. I started to fill my accounts with people that would inspire me to get me where I want to be whether it be financially or physically. This profound shift in the way I used social media actually got me fired up each day to work towards my goals.

Using social media as a tool of inspiration, I found myself excited to start making more money from each of my followers' inspirational posts. Whether it be from following tony-Robbins, accounts created by warren buffet followers, to people who were successful in YouTube and other online business platforms, I was motivated every time I logged in rather than leaving feeling worthless.

Who you follow matters and how you choose to use social media matters as well. If you choose comparison rather than inspiration, you will always feel like you are unworthy. If you view other's success as a motivator, you can choose to follow people that inspire you each and every day to get you where you want to go.

I challenge each and every one of you to align your goals with social media. Think hard about what you want to use it for. Is it a means of escape? Or is it a tool for you to get cracking on your goals. If you wish to be healthier, follow people who inspire you each day to start working out rather than those that posts photos that only serve to show off their physique. If you want to be richer, following successful people who teach you life principles to be wealthy, rather than accounts that merely show off their incredible wealth with things they buy and the branded stuff they own. If you goal is to be a better person, there are plenty of accounts that seek to inspire. Maybe Oprah Winfrey would be a good person to o follow, if she has an account.

Choose who you follow wisely because their daily posts will have a direct consequences to how you start seeing things around you.

Chapter 4:

How To Start Working Immediately

"There is only one way for me to motivate myself to work hard: I don't think about it as hard work. I think about it as part of making myself into who I want to be. Once I've chosen to do something, I try not to think so much about how difficult or frustrating or impossible that might be; I just think about how good it must feel to be that or how proud I might be to have done that. Make hard look easy." - Marie Stein.

Motivation is somewhat elusive. Some days you feel it naturally, other days you don't, no matter how hard you try. You stare at your laptop screen or your essay at the desk, willing yourself to type or write; instead, you find yourself simply going through the motions, not caring about the work that you're producing. You're totally uninspired, and you don't know how to make yourself feel otherwise. You find yourself being dissatisfied, discouraged, frustrated, or disappointed to get your hands on those long-awaited tasks. While hoping for things to change and make our lives better overnight magically, we waste so much of our precious time. Sorry to burst your bubble, but things just don't happen like that. You have to push yourself off that couch, turn off the phone, switch off Netflix and make it happen. There's no need to seek anyone's permission or blessings to start your work.

The world doesn't care about how tired you are. Or, if you're feeling depressed or anxious, stop feeling sorry for yourself while you're at it. It doesn't matter one bit. We all face obstacles and challenges and struggles throughout our days, but how we deal with those obstacles and difficulties defines us and our successes in life. As James Clear once said, "Professionals stick to the schedule, amateurs let life get in the way. Professionals know what is important to them and work towards it with purpose; amateurs get pulled off course by the urgencies of life."

Take a deep breath. Brew in your favorite coffee. Eat something healthy. Take a shower, take a walk, talk to someone who lifts your energy, turn off your socials, and when you're done with all of them, set your mind straight and start working immediately. Think about the knowledge, the skill, the experience that you'll gain from working. Procrastination might feel good but imagine how amazing it will feel when you'll finally get your tasks, your work done. Don't leave anything for tomorrow. Start doing it today. We don't know what tomorrow might bring for us. If we will be able even to wake up and breathe. We don't know it for sure. So, start hustling today. You just need that activation energy to start your chain of events.

Start scheduling your work on your calendar and actually follow it. We may feel like we have plenty of time to get things done. Hence, we tend to ignore our work and take it easy. But to tell you the truth, time flickers by in seconds. Before you know it, you're already a week behind your deadline, and you still haven't started working yet. Keep reminding yourself as to why you need to do this work done. Define your goals and get them into action. Create a clear and compelling vision of your work. You only achieve what you see. Break your work into small, manageable tasks so you stay motivated throughout your work procedure. Get yourself organized. Unclutter your mind. Starve your distractions. Create that perfect environment so you can keep up with your work until you're done. Please choose to be successful and then stick to it.

You may feel like you're fatigued, or your mind will stop producing ideas and creativity after a while. But that's completely fine. Take a break. Set a timer for five minutes. Force yourself to work on the thing for five minutes, and after those five minutes, it won't feel too bad to keep going. Make a habit of doing the small tasks first, so they get out of the way, and you can harness your energy to tackle the more significant projects.

Reward yourself every time you complete your work. This will boost your confidence and will give you the strength to continue with your remaining tasks. Don't let your personal and professional responsibilities overwhelm you. Help yourself stay focused by keeping in mind that you're accountable for your own actions. Brian Roemmele, the Quora user, encourages people to own every moment, "You are in full control of this power. In your hands, you can build the tallest building and, in your hands, you can destroy the tallest buildings."

Start surrounding yourself with people who are an optimist and works hard. The saying goes, you're the average of the five people you hang out with the most. So, make sure you surround yourself with people who push you to succeed.

No matter how uninspired or de-motivating it may seem, you have to take that first step and start working. Whether it's a skill that you're learning, a language that you want to know, a dance step that you wish to perfect, a business idea that you want to implement, an instrument that you want to master, or simply doing the work for anyone else, you should do it immediately. Don't wait for the next minute, the next hour, the next day, or the following week; start doing your stuff. No one else is going to do your work for you, nor it's going to be completed by itself. Only you have the power to get on with it and get it done. Get your weak spots fixed. In the end, celebrate your achievements whether it's small or big. Imagine the relief of not having that task up on your plate anymore. Visualize yourself succeeding. It can help you stay to stay focused and motivated and get your work done. Even the worst tasks won't feel painful, but instead, they'll feel like a part of achieving something big.

Remember, motivation starts within. Find it, keep it and make it work wonders for you.

Chapter 5:

How to Reprogram Your Mind for Success

Your routines are the things that drive you through life. Your routines are driven by your emotions. Your emotions are a sum of your past. Your past is a sum of incidents. These incidents may be related to a person or a thing, which in turn make your life exciting.

You start your day with a thought. A thought that wakes you up every day. A unique thought that everyone experiences every morning. These thoughts are the driving force for you to get up whether you like it or not.

These thoughts may be fear-driven or love memories. So your brain creates emotions in your subconscious mind which in turn dictates your daily tasks and routine.

You might be having doubts about a leave from a job that you might deserve because you can't get the doubt of getting fired out of your mind.

You might be remembering a loved one that you want to see today.

You may be hoping to get some good news today.

So you have a set routine every day, that you follow without even ever pondering on day-to-day life. And this is the ultimate failure of your purpose in life.

A routine that is not getting you forward in life isn't worth living with. But you are not able to think about it because your mind and your subconscious have taken over your body.

As all these obvious things are being stated, close your eyes, put some music on, shut the doors or sit on a bench in a quiet part. Tell your mind to get rid of those memories that drive your emotions. Leave your body motionless and try to take deep breaths.

As you start doing this, you will feel an immediate thought kick in your subconscious. Your mind will be making you feel like something is missing or if you had something to do.

This is an uncomfortable state of mind. But now is your time to be your own master. Tell your subconscious that it is your will that leads you, but not the emotions and your mind.

You have to realize the reality and make it seem more acceptable to your brain. You have to make it feel confident and feel that it is helping you to stay commited in any situation that comes across in your life.

You need to become conscious in this hectic world of involuntary unconsciousness.

You have to make yourself ready for the unpredictable future. Because if you are not ready for the future, you are still drowning in your past.

Everyone's past is toxic. Even good memories can be toxic. One might ask how.

The memories of the past either make your stay in the bed or they make you hope full of chances to come with luck. But luck is rarely lucky.

You cannot be a free man till you dive out of your personal reality that your brain has created to keep you in your comfort zone. You cannot become successful if you stay on your laptop or your phone interacting with the world via social media and emails.

You have to create your own environment by making new friends, taking new jobs, asking questions to your partner, making a change in your natural habitat.

Your mind is the curator of your environment and the people in it. So you have to change your environment by making your mind commit to your orders.

Give your mind a free space to rehabilitate and renew itself. Give it a chance to imagine new things. Make it wander off like a herd of cattle in the grasslands. Let it flow without any emotion, just to create enough space for new realities to pop in. As soon as it does, you will find yourself in a new realm of happiness and success.

Chapter 6:

How To Have The Best Day Everyday

We all have the power to create the kind of day we want to experience every time we go to sleep and wake up the next day.

It is normal to think that we will only have an amazing day when something good happens to us. We believe that good things only happen out of luck, chance, fate, or whatever, but we never think that we can create a good day just by our sheer desire to.

What the best day means to each of us may be different, some prioritise professional accomplishments as their measurement of a great day, some prioritise spending time with as many friends as possibly in a 24 hour period as one that is great. But when we depend on these circumstances, we are never really in full control of our day because bad things can always happen without a rhyme or reason. Our presentation that we have been working months on could suddenly be marred by a technical difficulty, or our friends could cancel on us last minute due to whatever reason.

What we thought would be our best day could turn out to be one filled with disappointments and maybe even loneliness.

I struggle with this all the time. Everytime i had built up the perfect day in my head, something always seem to go wrong somehow and I am left searching for a filler to cover that void. Through the fault of nobody but life getting the way, as it always does, I found out that if I always depended on others to give me the best day, that it rarely ever happens. Occasionally things work out great when I least expect it, but those occurrences are still out of my control.

It is only when we decide for ourselves that we can have the best day regardless of life inserting itself in, that we can truly enjoy every waking moment of our lives. By constantly reminding ourselves that we are grateful to be alive, to live each moment in the present, and to live as though tomorrow might never come, we can truly appreciate the little things in life that we often overlook. We have the best day because we believe that it is.

From the moment that we get out of bed, we appreciate the first breath we take, the first shower that we take, the first meal that we take, and all the little things that make up our wonderful day. Appreciating the fact that we are living with a roof over our heads, that we have clean water to drink, air conditioning to keep us cool, heaters to keep us warm, literally anything and everything around us, there is something to be grateful for.

When we start to notice that our life is truly amazing, we will never have to depend on other things or other people to make us have our best day. That is the kind of control we have over our day if we set it off on the right foot from the get-go.

It was only when I started being grateful for the fact that I am truly blessed with an amazing family, pet, friends, a house, that I realized i didn't need fancy party or fancy things to allow me to have the best day ever. Yes there are moments in life when we feel truly alive, those moments we will cherish and remember, but those moments are also few and far between. If we can take control of the other 364 days of the year, we would truly be the happiest people alive on this earth who are living their best days everyday.

Chapter 7:

How To Find Your Passion

Today we're going to talk about a topic that i think many of you are interested to know about. And that is how to find your passion.

For many of us, the realities of work and obligations means that we end up doing something we dislike for the money in the hopes that it might buy us some happiness. That sometimes we stop following our passion because maybe it does not exactly pay very well. And that is a fair decision to make.

But today, i hope to be able to help you follow at least one passion project at any point in your life in the hopes that it might help elevate your spirits, give your life more meaning, and help you live each day with a renewed drive and purpose.

You see, the world can be very dull if we chase something that we actually don't really feel attracted to. For example, when we are forced to do something out of sheer dread day in and day out, it will suck the living soul out of us and we will tend to fall into the trap of running an endless wheel with no hope in sight. When we chase material things for example, money or luxury products, we sell our soul to a job that pays well physically but not emotionally and spiritually. As a human being, we have traded our very essence and time, for a piece of paper or digital currency that serves no purpose than to enrich us externally. While it might feel good to be living comfortably, past a certain threshold, there is a point of diminishing returns. And more money just doesn't bring you that much joy anymore.

Yes you may have the fanciest, car, house, and whatever physical possessions you have. But how many of you have heard stories of people who have a lot of money but end up depressed, or end up blowing it all away because they can never spend enough to satisfy their cravings for physical goods and services. What these people lacked in emotional growth, they tried to overcompensate with money. And as their inner self gets emptier and emptier, they themselves get poorer and poorer as well.

On the flip side, many would argue that passion is overrated. That passion is nothing but some imaginary thing that we tell ourselves we need to have in order to be happy. But i am here to argue that you do not need to make passion your career in order to be happy.

You see, passion is an aspiration, passion is something that excites you, passion is something that you would do even if it does not pay a single cent. That you would gladly trade your time readily for even if it meant u weren't getting anything monetary in return. Because this passion unlocks something within you that cannot be explained with being awarded physical prizes. It is the feeling that you are truly alive and happy, you are so incredibly grateful and thankful to be doing at that very moment in time, that nothing else mattered, not even sleep.

To me, and I hope you will see this too, that passion can be anything you make it out to be. It can be something as simple as a passion for singing, a passion for creating music, a passion for helping others, passion for supporting your family, passion for starting a family, passion for doing charity work, passion for supporting a cause monetarily, or even a passion for living life to the fullest and being grateful each day.

For some lucky ones, they have managed to marry their passion with their career. They have somehow made their favourite thing to do their job, and it fulfills them each day. To those people, i congratulate you and envy you.

But for the rest of us, our passion can be something we align our soul with as long as it fulfils us as well. If we have multiple mouths to feed, we can make our passion as being the breadwinner to provide for our family if it brings us joy to see them happy. If we have a day job that we hate but can't let go off for whatever reasons, we can have a passion for helping others, to use the income that we make to better the lives of others.

And for those who have free time but are not sure what to do with it, to just simply start exploring different interests and see what hobbies you resonate with. You may never know what you might discover if you did a little digging.

What I have come to realize is that passions rarely stay the same. They change as we change, they evolve over time just as we grow. And many of the passions we had when we were younger, we might outgrow them when we hit a certain age. As our priorities in life change, our passions follow along.

In my opinion, you do not need to make your passion your career in order to be truly happy.. I believe that all you need is to have at least 1 passion project at any given point of time in your life to sustain you emotionally and spiritually. Something that you can look forward to on your off days, in your time away from work, that you can pour all your time and energy into willingly without feeling that you have wasted any second. And who knows, you might feel so strongly about that passion project that you might even decide to make it your career some day. The thing is you never really know. Life is mysterious like that.

All I do know is that chasing money for the wrong reasons will never net u happiness. But having a passion, whatever it may be, will keep you grounded and alive.

So I challenge each and everyone of you today to look into your current life, and see there are any bright spots that you have neglected that you could revive and make it your passion project. Remember that passion can be anything you make out to be as long as you derive fulfilment and happiness from it. Helpfully one that isnt material or monetary.

Chapter 8:

Get Rid of Worry and Focus On The Work

Worry is the active process of bringing one's fears into reality.

Worrying about problems halts productivity by taking your mind off the work in hand.

If you're not careful, a chronic state of worrying can lead you down a dark path that you might find hard to get out of.

Always focus on the required work and required action towards your dream.

Anything could happen, good or bad,

but if you remain focused and do the work despite the problems,

you will through with persistence and succeed.

Always keep your mind on the goal,

your eyes on the prize.

Have an unwavering faith in your abilities no matter what.

Plan for the obvious obstacles that could stand in your way,

but never worry about them until you have to face them.

Tackle it with confidence as they come and move forward with pride.

Problems are bound to arise.

Respond to them necessarily along the way, if they actually happen.

After all, most worries never make it into reality.

Instead focus on what could go right.

Focus on how you can create an environment that will improve your chances of success.

The Balanced Workaholic

You have the power over your own life and direction.

As children we dreamed big.

We didn't think about all the things that could go wrong.

As children we only saw the possibilities.

We were persistent in getting what we wanted no matter the cost.

As adults we need to be reminded of that child-like faith.

To crush worry as if it were never there.

To only focus on the possibilities.

You cannot be positive and negative at the same time.

You cannot be worrying and hopeful of the future.

You cannot visualise your perfect life while worrying about everything that could go wrong.

Choose one.

Stick to it.

Choose to concentrate on the work.

The result will take care of your worries.

Catch yourself when you feel yourself beginning to worry about things.

Instead of dwelling on the problem, choose to double down on the action.

Stay focused and steadfast in the vision of your ultimate goal.

The work now that you must do is the stepping stones to your success.

The work now must have your immediate attention.

The work now requires you to cast worry aside in favour of concentration and focus.

How many stepping stones are you away?

What is next?

Push yourself every single day.

Because only you have the power to create your future.

If not, things will remain the same as they have always been.

Always have a clearly defined goal,

A strong measure of faith,

And an equally strong measure of persistence and grit.

These are the ingredients to creating the life you want.

A life of lasting happiness and success.

Take control instead of accepting things as they are.

Reject anything else that is not the goal that you've set for yourself.

Whatever goal you set, ten times it, and focus on it every day.

The focus will keep your mind on the work until you succeed.

There will be no time to worry when you are too busy taking constant action.

Always have the belief In your heart and soul that you will succeed.

Never let a grain of doubt cast a shadow in your eventual path to victory.

Focus is key to all.

What you focus on, you will create.

Worrying is worse than useless,

it is DETRIMENTAL to your future.

Take control of your thoughts.

When worry pops it's ugly head, force it out with a positive thought of your future.

Don't let the negative illusions of worry live rent-free in your mind.

You are in control here.

Of what you watch,

What you read,

What you listen too

And what you think.

What you think of consistently will become.

Focus on what you want, and how to get there is crucial for lasting happiness and success.

Chapter 9:

How To Focus and Concentrate On Your Work

Today we're going to talk about a topic that I think everyone struggles with, including myself. Being able to sit in front of your computer for hours on end is not something that comes naturally to anyone, well not for me anyway.

Unfortunately, this is a skill that needs to be learned. And it is on some level crucial for our career success. So if this is something that you struggle with, then stick around for the rest of the video to learn how you can increase your level of concentration and to be more productive.

So what is focus and how do we get more of it?

The first thing we need to know is that focus is a state of mind. Without getting into too scientific terms, focus happens when our brains generate certain waves, I'm sure you've heard of alpha, theta, beta, waves. But to get to this state, we must give it some time. And the first step is to simply start sitting on your desk and practicing some deep breathing to get you prepared for that state. Close your eyes, just take some time to focus on your breath and nothing else. Feel your body calming down from a more excitable state, to one of more serenity and peace. Let go of any thoughts that come your way, whatever problems that crosses your mind, just let it flow away. If you need to take some time to do so right now, just pause the video and practice this deep breathing for yourself. For those that require a more holistic practice, you can check out my meditation link here, where you will be guided through a simple 10 min practice to get yourself in the right state of mind.

The Balanced Workaholic

The next thing we need to know about focus is that it requires us to be free from distraction. When we get interrupted in our workflow by distractions such as buzzing from our phones, social media, by other people, or even our pets, we break the momentum that we have so painstakingly built. According to Newton's Law: The law states that as object at rest will stay at rest, an object in motion will stay in motion unless acted on by a net external force. The same principle applies to our focus, when we break that motion, it will take an equal amount of energy to get us back on track again. So to save our brains from having to work extra hard to keep you concentrated, it is vital that we eliminate all possible sources of distraction that will pull us away from the state of focus. It is best that we set aside at least 1-2 hours of our time where nothing and no one can disturb us. Do not schedule your meals or coffee break in between those times of concentration as the same principle applies to those as well.

The final thing we need to know is that focus is a muscle, and the more that we train it each day, the easier it gets for us to get into that state. I believe that focus, as with anything else, requires a daily routine for us to get into the habit of being able to switch quickly from play to work. As you train yourself to be more focused, by first being more attentive to the various nuances of how to achieve focus, it will come more naturally to us if we keep applying the same practice for 10, 20, 30 days in a row. When we make a conscious effort to keep distractions away, when we find less excuses to wander around our work place, when we make it a point that we will do our very best to stay focused each and every day, it will come as no surprise that your levels of productivity and concentration will definitely increase. Our brain's capacity for staying in that state of mind will increase as well. And hopefully we will be more creative and innovative as a result.

I want to give you one more bonus tip to help you get the ball rolling, if you find you need an extra boost. That is to think of the rewards that being focused can get you. Try your best to visualise the benefits of being productive and getting your work out of the way, the time you will have after to do the things you enjoy, if work isnt one of them. The friends that you can see after the work is done, and how much time you won't have to waste being distracted and spending your whole day in front of your computer only to realise you only put in 2 hours of actual work in. Also think of the monetary rewards maybe of being focused, how much more money you can potentially be earning, or how many clients and business deals can you close if you just became more productive. You can even think of the intrinsic rewards of being focused, how proud would you be of yourself if you had actually done the 5-6 hours of work that you promised you would do.

So for those who are struggling with focus and concentration, I challenge you to take a look at the surroundings of your workplace... What can you do to minimise the distractions, and how can you get and stay in that focused state of mind for longer without letting your concentration drift away.

I believe that you can do anything that you set your mind to. So go out there and achieve focus like never before.

Chapter 10:
How To Find Motivation

Today we're going to talk about a topic that hopefully will help you find the strength and energy to do the work that you've told yourself you've wanted or needed to but always struggle to find the one thing that enables you to get started and keep going. We are going to help you find motivation.

In this video, I am going to break down the type of tasks that require motivation into 2 distinct categories. Health and fitness, and work. As I believe that these are the areas where most of you struggle to stay motivated. With regards to family, relationships, and other areas, i dont think motivation is a real problem there.

For all of you who are struggling to motivate yourself to do things you've been putting off, for example getting fit, going to the gym, motivation to stay on a diet, to keep working hard on that project, to study for your exams, to do the chores, or to keep working on your dreams... All these difficult things require a huge amount of energy from us day in and day out to be consistent and to do the work.

I know... it can be incredibly difficult. Having experienced these ups and downs in my own struggle with motivation, it always starts off swimmingly... When we set a new year's resolution, it is always easy to think that we will stick to our goal in the beginning. We are super motivated to go do the gym to lose those pounds, and we go every single day for about a week... only to give up shortly after because we either don't see results, or we just find it too difficult to keep up with the regime.

Same goes for starting a new diet... We commit to doing these things for about a week, but realize that we just simply don't like the process and we give up as well...

Finding motivation to study for an important exam or working hard on work projects are a different kind of animal. As these are things that have a deadline. A sense of urgency that if we do not achieve our desired result, we might fail or get fired from our company. With these types of tasks, most of us are driven by fear, and fear becomes our motivator... which is also not healthy for us as stress hormones builds within us as we operate that way, and we our health pays for it.

Let's start with tackling the first set of tasks that requires motivation. And i would classify this at the health and fitness level. Dieting, exercise, going to the gym, eating healthily, paying attention to your sleep... All these things are very important, but not necessarily urgent to many of us. The deadline we set for ourselves to achieve these health goals are arbitrary. Based on the images we see of models, or people who seem pretty fit around us, we set an unrealistic deadline for ourselves to achieve those body goals. But more often than not, body changes don't happen in days or weeks for most of us by the way we train. It could take up to months or years... For those celebrities and fitness models you see on Instagram or movies, they train almost all day by personal trainers. And their deadline is to look good by the start of shooting for the movie. For most of us who have day jobs, or don't train as hard, it is unrealistic to expect we can achieve that body in the same amount of time. If we only set aside 1 hour a day to exercise, while we may get gradually fitter, we shouldn't expect that amazing transformation to happen so quickly. It is why so many of us set ourselves up for failure.

To truly be motivated to keep to your health and fitness goals, we need to first define the reasons WHY we even want to achieve these results in the first place. Is it to prove to yourself that you have discipline? Is it to look good for your wedding photoshoot? Is it for long term health and fitness? Is it so that you don't end up like your relatives who passed too soon because of their poor health choices? Is it to make yourself more attractive so that you can find a man or woman in your life? Or is it just so that you can live a long and healthy life, free of medical complications that plague most seniors by the time they hit their 60s and 70s? What are YOUR reasons WHY you want to keep fit? Only after you know these reasons, will you be able to truly set a realistic deadline for your health goals. For those that are in it for a better health overall until their ripe old age, you will realize that this health goal is a life long thing. That you need to treat it as a journey that will take years and decades. And small changes each day will add up. Your motivator is not to go to the gym 10 hours a day for a week, but to eat healthily consistently and exercise regularly every single day so that you will still look and feel good 10, 20, 30, 50 years, down the road.

And for those that need an additional boost to motivate you to keep the course, I want you to find an accountability partner. A friend that will keep you in check. And hopefully a friend that also has the same health and fitness goals as you do. Having this person will help remind you not to let yourself and this person down. Their presence will hopefully motivate you to not let your guard down, and their honesty in pointing out that you've been slacking will keep you in check constantly that you will do as you say.

And if you still require an additional boost on top of that, I suggest you print and paste a photo of the body that you want to achieve and the idol that you wish to emulate in terms of having a good health and fitness on a board where you can see every single day. And write down your reasons why beside it. That way, you will be motivated everytime you walk past this board to keep to your goals always.

Now lets move on to study and work related tasks. For those with a fixed 9-5 job and deadlines for projects and school related work, your primary motivator right now is fear. Which as we established earlier, is not exactly healthy. What we want to do now is to change these into more positive motivators. Instead of thinking of the consequences of not doing the task, think of the rewards you would get if you completed it early. Think of the relief you will feel knowing that you had not put off the work until the last minute. And think of the benefits that you will gain... less stress, more time for play, more time with your family, less worry that you have to cram all the work at the last possible minute, and think of the good results you will get, the opportunities that you will have seized, not feeling guilty about procrastinations... and any other good stuff that you can think of. You could also reward yourself with a treat or two for completing the task early. For example buying your favourite food, dessert, or even gadgets. All these will be positive motivators that will help you get the ball moving quicker so that you can get to those rewards sooner. Because who likes to wait to have fun anyway?

Now I will move on to talk to those who maybe do not have a deadline set by a boss or teacher, but have decided to embark on a new journey by themselves. Whether it be starting a new business, getting your accounting done, starting a new part time venture.. For many of these tasks, the only motivator is yourself. There is no one breathing down your neck to get the job done fast and that could be a problem in itself. What should we do in that situation? I believe with this, it is similar to how we motivate ourselves in the heath and fitness goals. You see, sheer force doesn't always work sometimes. We need to establish the reasons why we want to get all these things done early in life. Would it be to fulfil a dream that we always had since we were a kid? Would it be to earn an extra side income to travel the world? Would it be to prove to yourself that you can have multiple streams of income? Would it to become an accomplished professional in a new field? Only you can define your reasons WHY you want to even begin and stay on this new path in the first place. So only you can determine why and how you can stay on the course to eventually achieve it in the end.

Similarly for those of you who need additional help, I would highly recommend you to get an accountability partner. Find someone who is in similar shoes as you are, whether you are an entrepreneur, or self-employed, or freelance, find someone who can keep you in check, who knows exactly what you are going through, and you can be each other's pillars of support when one of you finds yourself down and out. Or needs a little pick me up. There is a strong motivator there for you to keep you on course during the rough time.

And similar to health and fitness goal, find an image on the web that resonates with the goal you are trying to achieve. Whether it might be to buy a new house, or to become successful, i want that image to always be available to you to look at every single day. That you never forget WHY you began the journey. This constant reminder should light a fire in you each and everyday to get you out of your mental block and to motivate you to take action consistently every single day.

So I challenge each and every one of you to find motivation in your own unique way. Every one of you have a different story to tell, are on different paths, and no two motivators for a person are the same. Go find that one thing that would ignite a fire on your bottom everytime you look at it. Never forget the dream and keep staying the course until you reach the summit.

Distraction Is Robbing You

Every second you spend doing something that is not moving you
towards your goal, you are robbing yourself of precious time.
Stop being distracted!

You have something you need to do,
but for some reason become distracted by
other less important tasks and procrastinate on the important stuff.
Most people do it,
whether it's notification s on your phone or chat with colleges,
mostly less than half the working day is productive.

Distraction can be avoided by having a schedule
which should include some down time to relax
or perhaps get some of them distractions out of the way,
but time limited.

As long as everything has its correct time in
your day you can keep distraction from stealing too much of your time.
When your mind is distracted it becomes nearly impossible to
concentrate on the necessary work at hand.
Always keep this question in mind:
"is what I am about to do moving me towards my goal?"
If not, is it necessary?
What could I do instead that will?

It's all about your 24 hours.

Your actions and the reactions to your actions from that day,

good or bad.

By keeping your mind focused on your schedule that

moves you towards your goal, you will become resilient to distraction.

Distraction is anything that is not on your schedule.

You may need to alter that depending on the importance of the

intrusion.

Being successful means becoming single minded about your goal.

Those with faith do not need a plan b because they know plan A is the

only way and they refuse to accept anything else.

Any time you spend contemplating failure will add to its chances of

happening.

Why not focus on what will happen if you succeed instead?

Distraction from your vision of success is one of its biggest threats.

Blocking out distraction and keeping that vision clear is key.

Put that phone on flight mode and turn off the TV.

Focus on the truly important stuff.

If you don't do it, it will never get done.

The responsibility is all yours for everything in your life.

The responsibility is yours to block out the distractions and exercise

your free-will over your thoughts and actions.

By taking responsibility and control you will become empowered.

Refuse to let anyone distract you when you're working.

Have a set time in your schedule to deal with stuff not on the schedule.

This will allow you time to deal with unexpected issues without stopping you doing the original work.

The reality is that we all only have so much time.

Do you really want to waste yours on distractions?

Do you want to not hit your target because of them?

Every time you stop for a notification on your phone you are losing time from your success.

Don't let distraction rob you of another second, minute, hour or day.

Days turn to months and months turn to years don't waste time on distractions and fears.

CPSIA information can be obtained
at www.ICGtesting.com
Printed in the USA
BVHW041753131221
623925BV00014B/634